What I Taught MOM About Baseball

By Mitchell A. Rubenstein

AARON'S BOOKS

Ann Arbor, Michigan

Copyright © 1993 by Mitchell A. Rubenstein

All rights reserved. No part of this book may be reproduced or transmitted in any form by any means, electronic or mechanical, including, but not limited to photocopying, recording or by any informational storage or retrieval system — except by a reviewer who may quote brief passages in a review — without written permission from the publisher. For information contact Aaron's Books, P.O. Box 4241, Ann Arbor, Michigan 48106.

First Printing 1993

Although the author and publisher have exhaustively researched all sources to ensure the accuracy and completeness of the information contained in this book, we assume no responsibility for errors, inaccuracies, omissions or inconsistencies herein. Any slights of people or organizations are unintentional.

By offering a foreword, Cecil Fielder does not endorse any of the products displayed or contained herein.

Illustrations by Jeff Keyes
Editing by Maria-Elena Caballero-Robb

Dedicated to my mom.

Special thanks to my dad, my sister, Danny, Uncle Brian, and Fetch the Ump.

For help on *What I Taught Mom About Football,* thanks again Don Dorschel.

Foreword

When I was a child, my parents gave me a gift. This gift has nothing to do with physical ability, although that is part of my heredity, and it certainly has nothing to do with money, though if they could have, they would have given me that too. This gift could never be put in a package and placed under the Christmas tree, but it is as real as anything that I ever found there. In short, it made my life what it is today and without it I don't know where I would be.

The gift my parents gave me is my self-esteem. I don't know what doctors and other experts have to say about raising children. What I know and believe came from the two experts who raised me, and I think those people with all the letters after their names could probably learn a lot from them.

My parents never let me doubt that I was worthwhile and they never let me feel that I was any less of a person or less worthy because of any mistake I ever made. I don't want you to think that they never corrected me, or that they never punished me, because they did. But, even though I sometimes did bad things, they never made me feel that I was bad. They taught me that any mistake could be learned from and that I had a value inside that had nothing to do with any trophies or medals on the mantle. Some people may believe that the reason why I have accomplished what I have is because of my belief in myself. I do believe in myself; but only because my parents believed in me first.

I think that for a long time, I never considered any of this; but now that I have children of my own, I worry about what kind of parent I am. I only hope that I am a wise enough parent to give this gift to my children.

Cecil Fielder

Contents

1 Introduction

My friends and family know me as the ultimate baseball fanatic.

Mom blames Dad for my obsession. He took me out on our driveway and thrust balls, bats, and hockey sticks into my little hands before I could even walk. The story changes if you ask my older sister. She blames television. I frequently victimized her by dragging her to the T.V. to watch baseball when I was too young even to spell the names of the teams playing.

In my opinion, I became a true fan a few months after my sixth birthday. On a snowy April day in 1977, I was one of millions of Canadians who huddled around their T.V. sets to watch the birth of professional baseball in the city of Toronto. Eight years later, I cried myself to sleep after my beloved team fell one game short of going to the world championship.

It was strange that I grew up to be a baseball fan in a country that knew hockey first and nothing second. There was something about baseball that set it apart from other sports. I looked forward to the summer afternoons I spent with my dad at the old stadium by the lake: Together, we saw rookies like Cecil Fielder, who later blossomed into a super star. This was *our* team, and as we watched, we talked and waited anxiously for something exciting to happen so we could stand together and cheer.

Fifteen years after I watched their first game, I celebrated as my team was crowned world champion. I was so elated, I spent the night parading around my fraternity house draped in the Canadian flag. The joy I felt that night inspired me to write a book that would share my love of baseball with everyone. Fathers and sons, mothers and daughters, and sisters and brothers everywhere can now enjoy watching my favorite game. I hope people of all ages read *All About Baseball* and fall in love with a team of their own, at any level of baseball, and experience the gratification that I've gotten from my team.

Skim over *All About Baseball* once. Then, read it a second time to get comfortable with the information. When you feel comfortable enough, peruse the glossary. Here you'll find some of the more complicated baseball terms explained in a clear and straightforward manner. When you're watching baseball live, bring *All About Baseball* along for reference.

Most importantly, have fun! Enjoy learning about North America's favorite pastime. After reading and understanding some of the principles presented in this book, you can enjoy watching the game of baseball as much as millions of fans like myself do every year!

2 The Basics

What?

Baseball is a game with players and rules. It is played by catching, throwing, and hitting a little leather-covered ball with a long stick-like object called a *bat,* and by running along the boundaries of a diamond-shaped area within the field. Though it appears to be a boring game that requires a great deal of knowledge to understand, when explained correctly, baseball turns out to be a exciting and simple game filled with action.

Who?

Two teams play against each other. Each team is allowed to have nine players on the field when defending against scoring attempts by the other team. When trying to score, a team can have anywhere from one to four players on the field. Having extra players on the field—any more than nine or four, respectively—is illegal. Team members who are not playing stay in the *dug out* (see Where? below) or *bull pen* (see chapter "Here's the Pitch").

Teams have *managers* who call the shots during the games and practices. Managers are under constant pressure to win. As Dick Vitale once said, "Don't win and you get the ziggy, ziggy, ziggy." Two or more coaches assist the manager. Two of them serve as *base coaches,* and are permitted to occupy the *coaching boxes,* from where they guide their team when attempting to score. *Assistant coaches* aid the manager in all aspects of running his team.

Umpires are officials who patrol specific regions of the field and make judgments, referred to as *calls,* in order to make sure the players follow the rules. The importance of the umpires is discussed later on.

Why?

"My advice to you is not inquire why or whither, but just enjoy your ice cream while it's on your plate—that's my philosophy." - Thorton N. Wilder

Fans should just enjoy watching games—that's their ice cream, their objective. Teams, on the other hand, have the objective of scoring more runs (points) than the other team.

Where?

From overhead, the baseball field looks like a diamond, and has a *base* (a square, cushioned bag) located on each corner. The names of the bases are: *first base, second base, third base,* and *home plate.* Home plate must be flat against the ground.

Each base is 90 feet away from the next. The player trying to hit the baseball stands in the *batter's box.* There is one located on each side of home plate. The boxes next to first and third base are the coaching boxes.

When the player hits the baseball, he moves in a counter-clockwise direction inside the *base paths.* The base paths are imaginary straight lines that connect

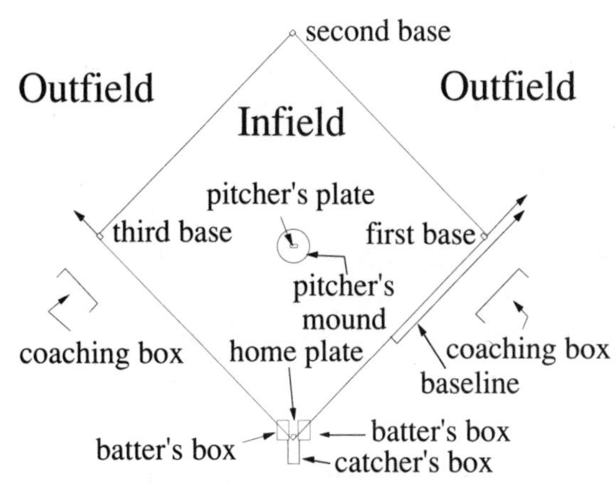

home plate to first base, first base to second base, second base to third base, and third base to home plate. He must safely touch first base, second base, and third base before finally touching home plate. In other words, he cannot run from first base to third base, or from second base to home plate.

An offensive player is never allowed to go more than three feet out side of these paths, unless he's avoiding a defensive player trying to catch the baseball, or when play has been stopped.

The part of the field located within the 90-square-foot diamond is called the *infield,* and the area of the field beyond the diamond is called the *outfield.* In the center of the infield is the *pitcher's mound.* From here one of the defensive team's players—the *pitcher*—throws the baseball to one of the offensive players—the *batter*—who tries to hit the baseball. These throws are called *pitches.* In the middle of the pitcher's mound is the *pitcher's plate,* or *rubber,* on which the pitcher stands. It is 60.5 feet away from home plate. Behind home plate is a tall barrier called a *backstop.* It stops baseballs that go past home plate.

Enclosing the outfield is a fence or wall that varies from

field to field in height, and distance from home plate. Some walls in professional *ball parks* (another word for stadiums) are so godzilla-like, they have nick-names like "The Green Monster" and "The Big Trash Bag".

In professional baseball the wall should be at least 325 feet from home plate when measured along straight lines extending from home plate through both first and third bases. These lines are called *foul lines*. Defining the foul lines are *foul poles,* located on each end of the *outfield wall.*

Out of Play

Shakespeare wrote, "Fair is foul, and foul is fair." With respect to baseball, this couldn't be further from the truth. Any baseball hit by a batter can be ruled either *foul* or *fair*.

In most cases, for a baseball to be considered fair, it must be hit within the foul lines. Any baseball hit outside of these lines is considered foul, and in all but a few situations, a *foul ball* will stop play. A baseball hit by a batter is foul if it goes outside of these lines before it passes first or third base.

A baseball that is touching one of the lines is fair, or playable. A baseball is also fair if it lands inside of the foul pole or hits one of these poles, but it is foul if it lands to the outside of the poles.

It may seem odd, but baseballs that go into foul territory aren't always foul. If a baseball touches one of the bases and then goes into foul territory, or touches somewhere in fair territory in the outfield before entering foul territory, then it is a *fair ball.*

Beyond foul territory is the area that is *out of play.*

This area would be the part of the ball park where the spectators sit. In parks without seats for spectators, this area would be designated by the umpire. In your local park, it could be the parking lot next to the baseball field. Once a baseball lands in the out of play area, it becomes a *dead ball,* at which point the play stops.

Meeting the Players

Offense

The only two offensive players are the batter and the *runner.* A batter becomes a runner if he hits the baseball and runs to or stops at an *open base* (a base with no other runner touching it).

Defense

The pitcher relies on eight other *fielders,* or players, who play defense against baseballs hit by the batter.

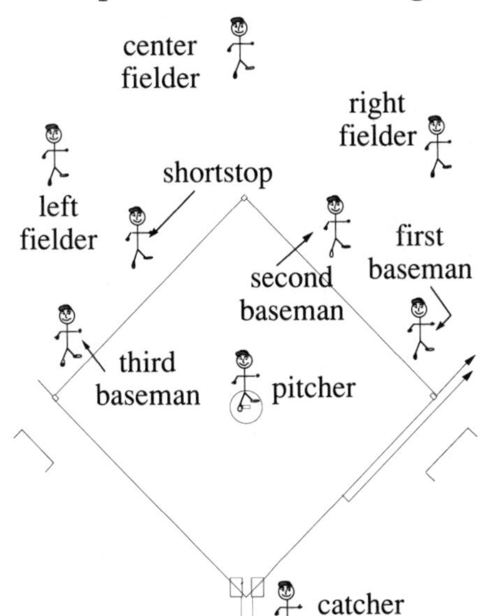

The *catcher* is a player who stands behind home plate to catch the baseballs the batter doesn't hit.

The *basemen* are responsible for catching baseballs thrown to their respective bases. Many times the shortstop catches baseballs thrown to second base.

An *infielder* plays a

defensive position in the infield, and an *outfielder* plays a defensive position in the outfield.

How?

"But now my task is smoothly done: I can fly, or I can run." - John Milton

Once some runners get on base, they can truly "fly." Yet, they still have to touch all of the bases in the correct order to reach home plate and score a run. Then their job is smoothly done.

Equipment

All members of a team are required to wear the same uniform. They all sport matching caps, pants, and tucked-in shirts. In other words, a player can't wear red while the rest of the team wears white. Players also wear shoes with cleats on the bottoms, and hard hats called *batting helmets* while batting.

Because catchers and umpires stand directly behind home plate, they use protective equipment to shield their faces and chests from high-speed baseballs. The catcher also wears protective equipment for his shins, called *shin guards*. He always wears his cap backwards. Umpires usually wear grey pants, a light blue shirt and a navy blue hat.

Most commonly bats are made out of wood or aluminum. Professional leagues only allow wooden bats because aluminum bats send the baseball too far.

Defensive players use a leather *glove* to catch the baseball. The size and thickness of a player's glove varies according to his defensive position. The catcher and first baseman use *mitts* which are more padded. If a player throws the baseball with his right hand then he wears the glove on his left, and vice versa.

Players can also wear gloves while batting called *batting gloves.* These gloves are thin and tight to the skin, and are used to give the batter a better grip on the bat.

Finally, you need that little leather-covered ball, known as the *baseball,* to play the game.

Always remember what Mao Tse-Tung said about baseball equipment, the day before he tried out for the pros:

"Weapons are an important factor in war, but not the decisive one; it is man and not materials that count."

From left to right: Top: first baseman's mitt, glove, base. Bottom: catcher's mitt, bat, baseball, catcher's mask, home plate.

When he broke his bat, he was cut from the team. Disgruntled, he went back to China to lead a revolution (not really).

Four Terms You Need To Know

An umpire calls *"safe"* when an offensive player touches and is allowed to stay on an open base. (Examples of this will be given throughout the book.)

When an offensive player is not permitted to stay on an open base, he is *out* and must leave the field. (A more complex definition will follow in a chapter called "You're Out.")

When a batter fails to hit a pitch the umpire rules is hitable, the umpire calls *"strike"*. Conversely, a ball is a pitch that the umpire rules not hitable. A more detailed definition of a ball and a strike will follow in Chapter 3, "Batter's Up."

When?

The game itself is divided into nine *innings* (six to nine innings in youth baseball). During an inning both teams have an opportunity to score. These innings have no time limit. Don't worry about the innings lasting for days or even hours. They end when each team has three outs against them.

The team designated as the *visiting team* bats first in every inning. If the *home team* is ahead at the end of eight and one-half innings, they already have enough runs to win the game.

If the score is tied at the end of nine innings, the two teams play *extra innings,* until one team is ahead at the end of a completed inning.

Catch 'n a Field

When a player makes a catch, he is said to be *fielding* the baseball. A player can use a glove to catch a baseball, but he cannot throw the glove off his hand to stop a baseball, nor use any part of his uniform. If he does, all runners on base will be awarded three bases. If a fielder throws his glove in the air in order to stop a home run from going over the outfield wall, all the runners are awarded four bases.

3 Batter's Up!

"In the long run, men hit only what they aim at." - Henry David Thoreau

Each time a batter steps into the batter's box to take his turn batting, he is said to be *up to bat.* The pitcher throws the baseball in the direction of home plate and the batter has the option of swinging at the pitch or not. Each team sends batters up to bat until their half-inning ends.

Types of Hits

Ulysses S. Grant told his troops, on a baseball break during the Civil War to "hit hard, hit fast, hit often."

When the batter hits the baseball it becomes one of five types of hits:

☞ *fly ball:* a baseball hit upward into the air.
☞ *ground ball:* a hit baseball that rolls on the ground.
☞ *line drive:* a baseball hit low and hard in the air.
☞ *bunt:* a baseball tapped rather than swung at.
☞ *home run:* a baseball hit over the wall. (For *inside the park home runs,* see the Glossary.)

When a batter gets one of these hits and is safe at first, second or third base, he is said to have gotten a *base hit.* If he only gets to first base, he is said to have hit a *single.* If he makes it to second base, he has hit a *double.* If he makes it to third base, he has hit a *triple.*

Calling Balls and Strikes

A strike is awarded if the batter swings and misses a pitch, or if the batter does not swing and the pitch is thrown in the *strike zone.* When a batter is in his *stance,* the strike zone is the area over home plate that begins half way between his waist and shoulders, and ends at the top of his knees.

A strike is also awarded if the batter hits a baseball that lands first in foul territory, or out of play, as long as it is not the third strike. There are only two cases in which a baseball hit into foul territory counts as a third strike. First, if a baseball is fouled directly back into the catcher's mitt, a strike will be called. This is called a *foul tip,* and can count as a first, second, or third strike. The other exception occurs when a batter with two strikes bunts a baseball foul .

"Viva la huelga [Long live the strike]!" said Cesar E. Chavez. It was the slogan of the United Farm Workers in the 1960's and is the slogan of all pitchers today.

The pitcher aims to throw strikes, not balls, to the batter. A ball is any pitch thrown out of the strike zone at which the batter does not swing. This rule insures that batters have good pitches to hit. A ball is also called when a pitcher makes an illegal pitch and there are no runners on base (for illegal pitches see Chapter 5 "Here's the Pitch."). If a batter is thrown four balls before he gets three strikes, he is allowed to run to first base. This is called a *base on balls,* or a *walk.*

The total number of balls and strikes the batter has against him while up to bat is called the *count.*

Our friend, the slow Haus Lingon in his batting stance.

The Batting Order

The manager of the team makes up a *batting order* of the nine players he has designated to play. Players must bat in that assigned order throughout the game. If they fail to do this, the player who missed his turn is out. A team sends up one batter at a time, and there is always one player on the field, or *on deck,* ready to bat after him. The batter after him is said to be *in the hole.*

Looking at home plate from the rubber, right-handed batters bat from the right side of home plate, and the lefties bat from the left side. Batters called *switch hitters* can bat from both sides of home plate. If a switch hitter is facing a right handed pitcher then he is most likely to bat as a left-handed batter, and vice versa.

In some leagues, the pitcher does not bat. Instead, the manager assigns a *designated hitter* to take his place in the batting order. Similar to the designated hitter, a *pinch hitter* may be substituted for any batter at any time in the game. **If any player is substituted out of a game, he cannot play for the remainder of that game.** His position in the batting order is taken over by the pinch hitter. His position in the field can be taken over by any player the manager chooses.

The Batter's Box

The batter must have both feet either inside or touching the batter's box when he is batting, and he must stay in the batter's box when the pitcher is about to pitch. He can only leave when the umpire declares, *"time"* (See Chapter 6 "The Umps"), thereby stopping play.

4 Rounding the Bases

Some runners are fast and some runners are slow, but no matter how fast or slow they are, they're all at the mercy of the rules that govern the rounding of the bases.

The Tag Out

When a fielder touches a runner with the baseball in his hand or glove, he is said to *tag* him. (He cannot have the baseball in one hand or his glove, and touch the runner with his free hand.) If a runner is advancing to a base to which he is not *forced* to run, a fielder must tag him in order to get him out. A runner is only forced to run if there are runners trying to advance from preceding bases.

Unless play has been stopped, any time a runner is not on a base, he can be tagged out. A runner **is** allowed to touch and run past first base without being tagged out, as long as he

Preceeding runners are always allowed to force runners off the bases

runs straight past or on the right side of the base. If the batter touches first base and then runs towards second base, he can be tagged out.

Stealing Bases

Runners try to *steal* bases. This happens when a runner runs to the open base ahead of him just as the pitcher is about to throw the baseball to the batter. When there are runners on two bases, a team may try a *double steal.* A runner on third base can even steal home plate.

A runner is allowed to step off a base when he waits for a pitch to be thrown. This is called a *lead* or *leading off.* If a runner takes a lead, the baseball can be thrown to a fielder guarding the base from which the runner is leading off in attempt to tag him out. Since stealing bases is such a big part of baseball, catchers need to have strong and accurate arms to throw the baseball to a base a runner is attempting to steal.

Runners may also try to advance to the next base if a pitcher throws a *wild pitch* or a *passed ball.* A wild pitch is a pitch thrown away from home plate that the catcher has no way of catching, and a passed ball is a pitch the catcher should be able to catch but does not.

Caught in a Pickle

Sometimes a runner gets caught running between two bases. This is called a *run down* or *pickle.* It begins when a runner attempting to get to a base finds a fielder waiting to tag him out. He may then try to run back to the base he came from, only to find the baseball has been thrown back to the fielder at that base. By this time a run down has begun, and the runner desperately tries to get back to one of the bases before the fielders can close in on him. He can only be called out if he runs off the base paths or is tagged out.

Caught in a pickle, he has "no where to run to."

Awarding an Extra Base

Umpires sometimes award runners extra bases. If the baseball rolls or bounces out of play, any runners on base will be allowed to advance one base. If, for example, a defensive player fields a ground ball and throws it past the first baseman, and out of play, the runner is safe at first base and is allowed to advance to second base. This rule is intended to prevent runners from scoring if the baseball is irretrievable. To prevent these types of throws, known as *over throws,* managers instruct certain fielders to back up other fielders at each base. This means players will run to stand somewhere behind a fielder expecting a throw.

Awarding Two Bases

The runners will also be awarded two bases if a fielder catches a ground ball, and throws the baseball directly out of play when there are runners on the bases.

Ground Rule Doubles

A ground rule double is ruled if the batted baseball lands anywhere in fair territory and bounces out of play, if it is deflected into the stands by a fielder, or if it becomes lodged somehow in a fence or bushes. The batter and runners who are on base at the time will be allowed to advance two bases.

What A Runner Can't Do

The runner can't intentionally touch the baseball or any of the fielders once the baseball is in the field of play. If he does, he's out. However, a runner can touch a fielder when he is trying to run to a base a fielder is blocking. Yet, if any fielder's throw hits a runner, and the fielder is clearly at fault, the play continues.

There can be only one player standing on a base at a time. Therefore, if two runners are standing on the same base, the one who arrived first is safe, and the one who arrived second must only be touched by a fielder holding the baseball to be called out.

Fan Interference

If spectators interfere with a baseball that is still in play, the umpire awards the runners the number of bases they would have advanced had there been no interference. Most fans interfere by reaching onto the field to catch fair baseballs that have rolled into foul territory.

5 Here's the Pitch

A team relies on their pitcher to help keep the other team from scoring. Every team hopes their pitcher will throw his best stuff (pitches), every time he is out on the mound.

Painting The Corners

Besides the middle of the strike zone, there are four basic locations around home plate where the pitcher can throw his pitches:

- ☞ high, at the top, or above, the strike zone,
- ☞ low, on the bottom, or under the strike zone,
- ☞ *inside,* the side of home plate closest to the batter,
- ☞ *outside,* the side of home plate away from the batter.

When a pitcher is at his best, he is able to throw the baseball into these areas where it is tough for the batter to hit, while at the same time keeping the baseball in the strike zone. When a pitcher is able to do this, he is said to be *painting the corners.*

Tough Pitches To Hit

One of the most confusing aspects of baseball for beginning fans is the lingo used to describe pitching. Fans and batters sometimes ponder these questions: Are pitchers who throw *screw balls,* really carpenters?. Are pitchers who throw the *gas* or *heater,* really putting fire on the baseball?. Are pitchers who throw *curve balls,* really tossing the end of a sidewalk? Some batters may think so, because when a pitcher is throwing well, he can make it really tough to hit the baseball.

"Try and hit the heater, meat!"

The Balk

There are specific rules that a pitcher must follow while pitching. When he breaks these procedural rules, he is said to balk. Here are his rules:

- ☞ he must be holding the baseball when he steps on the rubber,
- ☞ he may not drop the baseball, even by accident, once he has it in his hand,
- ☞ he may not make any motion that simulates a pitch without pitching the baseball,
- ☞ he must step toward the base he is throwing to, when attempting to pick off a runner (throw to a fielder to tag a runner out),

☞ he is never allowed to fake a throw to first base,
☞ he may only legally fake a pitch to second and third base when there are runners on those bases.

If runners are on base and any of the above rules are violated by the pitcher, the runners are automatically awarded a base. If no one is on base, the batter is awarded a ball. The batter is never awarded a base. If the batter hits the baseball and reaches a base after the pitcher balks, the play stands and the batter gets whatever base he earned on his hit. If runners are on base at the time the batter gets the hit, they are allowed to stay on the bases they earned on the play, as long as they all advanced at least one base.

Talk or Get Yanked

Once a game begins, the manager or pitching coach, can go talk to the pitcher on the mound only once per inning. If a manager or pitching coach from the same team visits the mound twice in an inning, the pitcher has to be removed from the game. Some pitchers get tired late in the game and don't pitch as well as they have earlier in the game. In this case, the manager may choose to replace a pitcher. Throwing too many

"We are in the ninth and here comes Mom to shut 'em down."

pitches in one game can also increase a pitcher's risk of injury.

If the manager wants to take his pitcher out of the game, he has the option of selecting a pitcher from his bull pen, which is where his extra pitchers sit. These other pitchers are called *relief-pitchers* or *relievers.* Once a new pitcher has come into the game, he must pitch to at least one batter before he can be replaced, unless he gets injured or the inning ends with a player being caught stealing. A replaced pitcher cannot return to pitch again in the game once he is removed.

Relief pitchers warm up in the bull pen during the game in case they are called upon to pitch. If a pitcher gets injured and a new pitcher has to be called in to take his place, the umpire will allow the new pitcher to throw as many warm-up pitches as he needs.

In the 'Pen'

Like bulls in a pen, the relievers are ready to explode onto the field. Here are the different types of relievers:

- ☞ The *closer* comes in late in the game to try to get the final few batters out. He is a hard thrower who faces only a few batters (usually in the ninth inning). He is able to pitch in almost every game.
- ☞ The *set up man* comes in before the closer and also has the job of getting only a few batters out. This man sets the table for the closer to come in and eat the meal. The set up man is most likely to pitch in the seventh or eighth inning. The last three innings are considered *late innings.*
- ☞ The *middle reliever* comes in to replace the starting pitcher in the *early innings* (first, second, or third)

or *middle innings* (fourth, fifth, and sixth). He is expected to pitch as many innings as necessary until the manager is ready to bring in the set up man or the closer.

Holding the Runner

It is important to note that a pitcher can throw the baseball to any base as often as he'd like, as long as the base he's throwing to is occupied by a runner. A pitcher does this to prevent a runner from getting too big of a lead toward the next base.

Getting Rid of the Baseball

If there are no runners on the bases, a pitcher has twenty seconds to pitch the baseball after receiving it from the catcher. If he doesn't, the batter is awarded a ball. If the pitcher intentionally delays the game more than once, he will be ejected by the umpire.

Beanball

A pitch that hits a batter is called a *beanball.* A pitcher is not allowed to throw the baseball at the batter intentionally. If the pitch hits the batter out of the strike zone, he is awarded first base. If the home plate umpire thinks the pitcher threw at the batter intentionally, he can eject the pitcher. He can also eject the manager if he believes the manager has instructed the pitcher to throw at the batter.

Doctoring the Baseball

Doctored baseballs afford the pitcher a better grip, allowing him to put extra spin on his pitches, making it tougher for the batter to hit. A pitcher may not deface the baseball in any way or put any foreign substances onto the baseball that would give him an advantage in throwing it. He must never throw a spit ball, shine ball, mud ball, sandpaper ball, or an ear wax ball. Not even a bubble gum ball is allowed. Finally, at no time may a pitcher throw the once popular and now infamous, "Dr. Hiram P. McGillicutty's baldness-tonic-and-liver-potion ball." The pitcher may, however, use rosin bags and saw dust to prevent his hands from sweating.

The Science of Pitching

6 The "Umps"

The umpires, or *umps,* make sure the rules of the game are followed correctly. The chief umpire is the home plate umpire. He is responsible for overseeing a host of tasks. He stands behind the catcher to call runners safe or out at home plate. He also distinguishes balls from strikes, and keeps the batter's count. In addition, he may stop the game in the event of heavy rain or a player's injury. If he wants play to be stopped for whatever reason, he will declare, "time." Once play has recommenced, the umpire will declare, *"play ball."*

"A hard rain's a-gonna fall"
— Bob Dylan

The *field umpires* assist the home plate umpire and are second in command. These umpires make the calls at the bases, and sometimes assist the home plate umpire in determining whether or not a batter has swung.

Frequently, players, managers, or coaches argue with the umpires over a call. Even the fans yell at the umpires from time to time. Yet no matter how angry they get, no one may ever touch an umpire or they will be ejected from the game. It rarely pays for anyone to argue with an umpire because the ump always wins.

Strike

Time

Safe

Out

7 You're Out!

"You're out," are two words a fielder loves to hear. Throughout an inning, he'll do anything he can, within the rules, to get players from the other team out.

Three Usual Ways

The team playing defense has many ways to get outs. The most exciting for the fans is the strike out. When the pitcher rings up three strikes against the batter, he is credited with the out.

Another method is catching fly balls. A batter is called out if a fielder catches a fly ball before it hits the ground, and holds it long enough for the umpire to see that it has been caught. This only holds true if the baseball has not touched any objects, umpires, or opposing players.

A third way of getting an out is the ground ball out or *ground out*. In this case, a fielder fields a ground ball and throws it

A tough way to catch a flyball!

to the fielder touching first base, before the runner gets there. This is also known as a *force out* and can be made at any base, including home plate, as long as the preceding bases are occupied by runners. If all bases are occupied, the bases are said to be *loaded,* and there is a force out at every base.

Once a player is called out, he must leave the field immediately. If a player called out interferes with a fielder trying to get an additional out, the runner not yet out will be called out as well.

The Double-Play

A *double-play* is one sequence of play in which two offensive players are called out.

The most common double play is the ground-ball double play. This occurs when two force outs result from a ground ball. Fielders can also make fly ball double-plays. The rules of baseball allow for a runner to stand on their base and *tag up,* or run to unoccupied bases ahead of them once a fly ball has been touched by a fielder in fair or foul territory. If a runner leaves the base before the baseball is caught, the fielder must only throw it back to any player touching the base from which the runner left to get both the runner and the batter out.

Other Ways For Players to Be Called Out

There are three other ways a batter may be called out. First, a batter may not touch the baseball after it has been hit into the field of play. Second, the batter may not make contact or interfere with the catcher or other fielders. Finally, the batter may not try to use the bat to hit the baseball a second time. If he drops the bat, though, hitting the baseball by accident, the umpire will allow the play to continue.

The Infield Fly Rule

Similar to the fly ball out is the *Infield Fly Rule.* This rule states that if a batter hits a catchable fly ball inside the infield with fewer than two outs and with runners on first and second base, or with the bases loaded, he is out. Whether the fielder catches the fly ball or not doesn't matter. This rule is intended to prevent fielders from intentionally dropping the baseball to set up easy double-plays.

Appeal Play

Sometimes runners fail to touch one or more of the bases they have passed. For example, a batter might hit the baseball and advances to third base, but in haste, miss touching first base. In order for him to avoid getting called out, he must return along the base paths to touch first base. He does not automatically get to go back to third base. If the runner does not run back to touch first base, a fielder can throw the baseball back to a player touching first base to get him out. This is called an *appeal play.* If the runner misses home plate, he has to be tagged out, unless he leaves the field. In this case, the fielder only has to touch home plate while holding the baseball.

Base Running Blunders

In the event that a runner passes another runner along the base paths, he will be called out. This may sound unlikely, but it has happened, costing teams victories in big games. In one championship game, a batter came to bat in the ninth inning with two outs and the bases loaded. His team was trailing by three runs. He hit a long home run, which he thought would be a dramatic game winning *grand slam* (a home run hit with the bases loaded). Unfortunately, in his exuberance, he ran past one of the runners on his team and was called out by the umpire. Only the two runners who touched home plate before he was called out counted as runs. His team lost by one run.

The Third Strike Rule

There is one exception to the rule that three strikes make an out: the long-standing *third-strike rule.* This rule states that if first base is unoccupied, or if first base is occupied with two outs and the catcher drops the third strike, the batter may try to advance to first base, as though he hit the baseball.

"Not this time, Rook"

8 Statistics

Every batter measures the accomplishments of his season, or the playing year, by his *numbers* at the plate, also called *statistics*. Statistics are computed throughout the season, unless denoted as life-time statistics. Life-time statistics are computed for all seasons.

At Bat

An *at bat* is chalked up any time a batter gets a base hit, gets out, reaches base on an *error* (a blundered defensive play by a fielder), or reaches base on a *fielder's choice*. A fielder's choice is a play in which a batter reaches base because a fielder has chosen to get a preceding runner out rather than throwing to first base to get the batter out. An at bat is never recorded when a batter is awarded first base by the umpire. As well, the *sacrifice* play does not count as an at bat. A sacrifice play happens when a batter intentionally sacrifices his chances to get on base so that other runners can advance.

Batting Average

The number most players would like to see as high as possible is their batting average. A players batting average is computed by dividing the total number of base hits and home runs by his at bats.

For example, if a player has two hundred at bats and he hits the baseball fifty times, his batting average would be 50 divided by 200, or .250.

RBI

Another important number for a batter is the *RBI,* or *runs batted in.* Any time runners on base reach home plate due to his hit, the batter is credited with RBIs. If, for example, there are two runners on base, and a batter gets a hit that scores both runners, he gets two RBIs. A batter can also get a RBI for walking with the bases loaded. This would be a bases loaded walk forcing in a run.

RBIs can also come from sacrificing to score runs. If, for example, a batter hits a ground ball out, and a runner on third scores, he has officially sacrificed himself to get an RBI.

Hungry for some RiBIes

During a ground ball sacrifice play, if there are two outs and a runner scores before the third out is made, the run counts and the team's half-inning ends (except in the case of a force out).

A RBI sacrifice fly can only occur with fewer than two outs.

Home Run

"Not only do I knock 'em out, I pick the round." - Cassius Clay

The home run counts as an automatic run for the team and an RBI for the batter. Any runners on base score as well, and the batter gets RBIs for all of these runners.

Home runs are most often hit by strong and powerful hitters. A home run is, without a doubt, the most exciting play in baseball. Baseball fans love nothing more than to see their team, trailing late in the game, score a game-winning home run.

Runs Scored

This is the total number of runs a player scores during the season. Every time a runner crosses home plate safely, he is credited with a run scored.

Slugging Percentage

A batter's slugging percentage is computed by giving him one point for all the singles he has hit, two points for all the doubles, three points for all the triples, four points for all the home runs, and dividing the total combined number by his total number of at bats. For example, if a batter had 50 singles, 20 doubles, 10 triples, 10 home runs, and 300 at bats, his slugging percentage would be 50+40+30+40 = 160 divided by 300, or a .533 slugging percentage.

On Base Percentage

On base percentage is computed by dividing a batter's total number of hits, walks, and times hit by a pitch by his total number of at bats, walks, times hit by a pitch and sacrifices. A high on base percentage means a player will have more chances to score runs.

Fielding Average

This statistic is computed for a fielder by dividing his total number of *put-outs* and *assists* by his total number of put-outs, assists and errors.

Strike Outs and Walks

Statistics are kept for the total number of strike-outs and walks a pitcher throws and a batter is credited with.

Stolen Bases

Statistics are kept for the total number of stolen bases a player has.

Caught Stealing

Wins, Losses, and Saves

Starting pitchers look to win games. Relief pitchers look to save games.

A *win* is credited to the pitcher, who was the last player to pitch for his team when their winning run was scored. This can be either a starter or a reliever. A *loss* is credited to any pitcher who allows the opposing team to score enough runs to win the game. If a pitcher leaves the game while his team is ahead 4-2, he does not get the win if they end up winning 5-4. Instead, the pitcher who was in the game right before the winning run, becomes the new *pitcher of record* (the name given to the pitcher who records the win or the loss). In this case, the first pitcher is said to be *off the hook.*

Starting pitchers rely on the bull pen to hold leads once they have left the game. Any time a relief-pitcher enters the game in which his team leads by three or fewer runs, or with the potential tying run on base, at the plate, or on deck, and finishes the game without giving up more than two runs, he is said to have pulled off a *save.* A relief-pitcher can also get a save if he enters a game with more than a three run lead, and pitches well for at least three innings. Only one save can be credited to a single pitcher in a game.

Earned Runs versus Errors

An error is attributed to a fielder if he blunders a play, making him responsible for an out not being recorded. For example, if a baseball is hit easily to the shortstop, and he throws it wild to first base allowing the batter to reach first safely, the shortstop receives an error. Errors are ultimately determined by an *official scorer.*

An earned run is any run given up by a pitcher that is not the result of an error.

ERA

A pitcher is also measured by his *ERA,* or *earned run average.* An ERA is computed by multiplying the total number of earned runs given up by a pitcher during the season by the number of innings (six to nine, depending on the league), and then dividing the total by the number of innings the pitcher is in the game. For example, if a pitcher gives up 70 earned runs while pitching 180 innings in nine inning games, his ERA would be computed: 70 runs, multiplied by 9 (innings) divided by 180= 3.50 ERA. If a pitcher's ERA is low—in the high two's or low three's—he is contributing to his team's chance of winning by allowing as few runs as possible.

9 Scoring

Scoring can be a fun part of baseball. Bring your score book along to a game and begin to learn baseball's intellectual side. Don't forget to always score in the diagram under the appropriate inning and to the right of the player who is batting.

Recording Batters Reaching Base

The possible ways for a batter to reach base are:

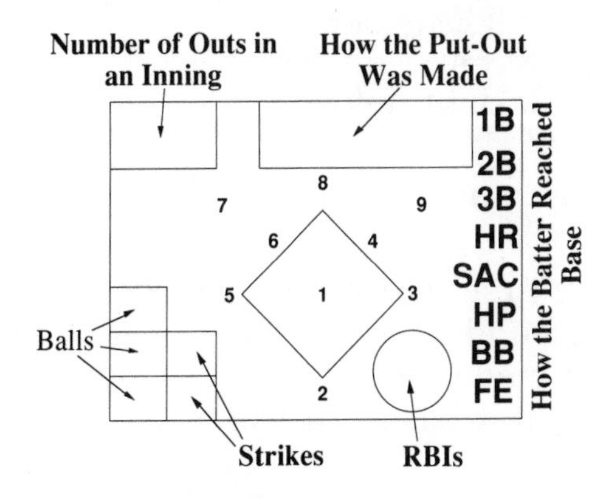

1B: one-base hit
2B: two-base hit
3B: three-base hit
HR: home run
SAC: sacrifice
HP: hit by pitcher
BB: base on balls
FE: fielder's error

Follow these steps:

1) Circle one of these to designate how the batter reached base.

2) Draw a line from home plate around the diamond to the base the batter reached.

3) When a runner reaches home plate, solidly color the

entire diamond.

- ☞ record RBIs scored by the batter in the circle on the diagram (including one for the batter if he scores)
- ☞ record balls on the batter in the column with three boxes
- ☞ record strikes on the batter in the column with two boxes

Recording Outs

A number is assigned to each defensive player's position

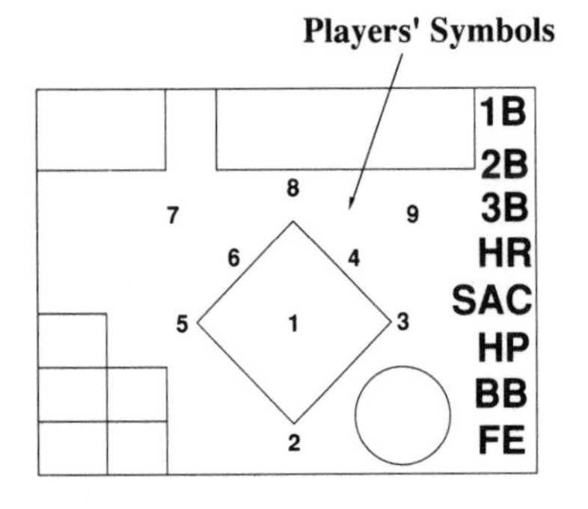

1 pitcher
2 catcher
3 first baseman
4 second baseman
5 third baseman
6 shortstop
7 left fielder
8 center fielder
9 right fielder

Record how all outs were made in the box in the upper right corner of the diagram:

1) For ground ball outs, first record the number of the fielder who caught the ground ball and then record the number of the player who made the out. An out made by the third baseman to the first baseman would be scored as 5-3.

2) For fly ball outs, write the letter 'F' next to the number of the fielder who caught the baseball (e.g. F-9).

3) For line outs, write the letter 'L' next to the number of the fielder who caught the baseball (e.g. L-6).

4) For double play outs follow the rules that apply to 1,2 and 3 and record the outs in the order they were made.

The most common double play is the 6-4-3, or the baseball thrown from the shortstop to the second baseman to the first baseman to record outs at second and first base.

Don't forget to record which out the player made in each inning in the box in the upper left corner of their diagram.

Recording Other Plays

For a swinging strike out write K

For a called strike out write Kc

For a fielder's choice write FC, then the number of the fielder who first touched the baseball.

For a sacrifice fly write SF, then the number of the fielder who caught the baseball.

For an error write E next to the number of the fielder who made the error.

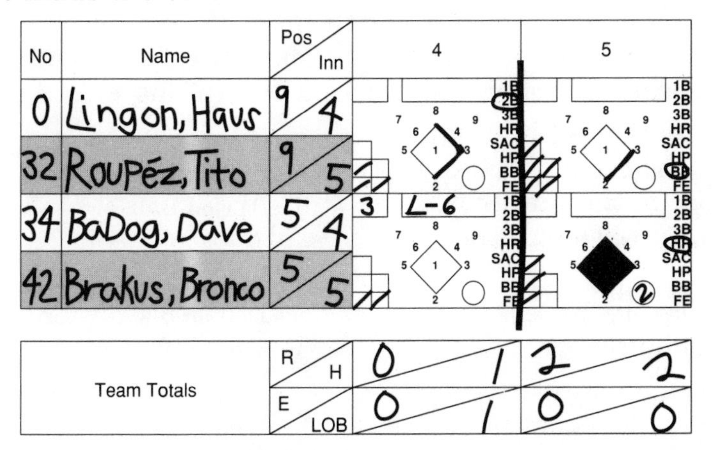

R= Runs H=Hits E=Errors LOB= # of runners Left on Base
For team totals, write down the number that has occured in each inning for all four statistics.

Scoring A Typical Game

With two outs in the fourth inning, Haus Lingon hit the baseball all the way to the wall on a 2-1 count (balls are always said before strikes). Unfortunately, he was so slow that he only made it to second base. Dave BaDog batted next hoping to bring Lingon home with an RBI hit. This was not to be, as he lined out to the shortstop. No other batters hit the baseball or reached base in the inning, and it ended with Haus still on second base.

In the next inning the manager was looking for a little more speed in his line up, so he opted to bring in the speedy Tito Roupéz to bat for the slow Haus. After a lengthy at bat, Tito walked after his count went to three and two. After losing confidence in Dave's ability to hit with runners on base, the manager opted to bring in the dangerous Bronco Brakus to pinch hit. The pitcher knew that Bronco had home run power, so he nervously threw him three balls. On the fourth pitch Bronco parked the baseball over the outfield fence for a two run home run. The next two batters got out and the inning ended with no one on base.

Other Scoring Symbols

HP=Hit by Pitcher
ERA=Earned Run Average
HB=Hit Batter
SAC=Sacrifice
WP=Wild Pitch
INT=Interference
BK=Balk
BB=Base on Balls
C/S=Caught Stealing
IW=Intentional Walk
BF=Batters Faced
ER=Earned Run

PB=Passed Ball
IP=Innings Pitched
SB=Stolen Base
FE=Fielder's Error
DP=Double Play
PO=Put Outs
S=save
A=Assists
W=Won
L=lost

10 Extra Innings

In his book written in 1954 entitled God's Country and Mine, Jacques Barzum wrote, "Whoever wants to know the heart and mind of America had better learn baseball, the rules and realities of the game—and do it first by watching some high school or small-town teams." I hope my book encourages all those have who have read it, to act on those words. The magnitude of baseball does not exist because of teams or players, it exists because of fans.

Baseball is about the proud father who clutches the hand of his son, as they walk inside the ball park together for the first time. The father has waited a lifetime to take his son to a ball game, just as his father had taken him many years before. For the son, it's a chance to watch his "heroes to be" play.

Baseball is about mom, whose heart breaks for her son every time he loses a game.

The game is not about how often a player hits the baseball, for a man is considered a legend if he manages to hit the baseball only four out of every ten times. It's about the moment when a player gets an important hit that makes baseball so special.

I'll always remember the day I spent with my dad at the old stadium by the lake, when we watched our team play there for the last time. As the final home run sailed past our heads, I knew we would never again sit there together to watch a game. Now, that game has become a faded memory, but I can still remember the game winning home run and how happy it made my dad and I feel.

As players come and go every year and new stadiums replace old ones, it is the fans who remain stable. I'll always have my dad, and he'll always have me, and together we will always have baseball.

Glossary

ace The best starting pitcher on a team. The blue birds have their ace pitching today.
appeal play A play in which the defense throws the baseball back to a base to check if a runner missed touching the base.
assist A statistic with which a fielder is credited when he throws the baseball to another fielder who in turn makes an out.
at bat The statistical term used to calculate batting average, arrived at by totaling the number of times a batter gets a base hit, reaches base on an error, or a fielder's choice, or gets out.
backstop A tall barrier behind home plate. *His foul ball hit the backstop.*
balk An illegal pitch thrown by a pitcher (see chapter 5 "Here's the Pitch").
ball 1. A pitch the umpire says is not hitable by the batter. 2. Short for a baseball.
ball park A baseball field.
base The square bag located on each corner of the diamond-shaped playing field.
base coaches The coaches permitted to occupy the coaching boxes when their team is batting.
base on balls The batter's privilege of advancing to first base after the pitcher throws four balls.
base paths The imaginary straight lines that connect home plate to first base, first base to second base, second base to third base, and third base to home plate.
base rap Slang for a base hit. *Roberto hit a solid base rap to left field.*
base runner Slang for runner.
base theft Slang for stolen base. *Devon just pulled off his third base theft of the game.*
baseball 1. A round ball covered by leather. 2. A game.
baseman Fielders that position themselves near first, second, third base.
bases juiced Slang for bases loaded. *Oh my, Kirby's coming up to bat with the bases juiced.*
bases loaded When there are runners occupy first, second and third bases.
bat A long stick-like object used by the batter to hit the baseball.
batter The offensive player who tries to hit the baseball.
batter's box The area next to home plate where the batter stands to hit the baseball.

batter's helmet A hard hat worn by the batter while batting.
batter's stance The position the batter uses while batting.
batter-runner The term used for a batter running to first base.
battery The name given to the pitcher-catcher combination. *Juan and Pat are an impressive battery.*
batting glove The thin-to-the-skin gloves the batters wear on their hands while batting.
batting order The assigned order in which the batters hit in during the game.
behind the dish The area where the catcher is positioned behind home plate. *Ernie is playing solid behind the dish.*
bloop single blooper. A softly hit fly ball that lands in the outfield. *Manny hit yet another blooper.*
blue Slang for umpire.*"Open your eyes, Blue!"*
brush off A pitch thrown to the inside of home plate.
boot An error in which a fielder misplays a ground ball, and accidently kicks it. *Another boot by Kelly, on what should have been an easy play.*
button The half inning when the home team bats
bull pen The area where the relievers sit when they prepare to go into the game. *Duane is set to come out of the pen to pitch in the eighth inning.*
bunt 1. A hit in which a batter holds the bat out for a pitch so he can tap it. 2. The action of bunting.
call An umpire's judgement based on the rules.
can-o-corn Slang for an infield fly. *Alfredo just hit another can-o-corn.*
catcher The defensive player who stands behind home plate to catch the pitches that are not hit by the batter.
caught looking Slang for a strike out. *Wade was caught looking for the third time this game.*
center field The middle part of the outfield.
center fielder A defensive player who is positioned in the center field.
change up A pitch that starts high and comes in low to a batter.
cheat off the bag, -ing To stand away from a base before a pitch. *Ricky was caught cheating off the bag.*
check swing A half swing at a pitch. *Looks like Paul managed to check his swing to avoid strike three.*
chopper A hard bouncing ground ball. *The chopper went right over Tony's head.*
clean-up hitter The batter who hits fourth in the batting order. *Dave was the best clean up hitter in the league last year.*
closer A hard-throwing relief-pitcher who comes in late in the game to pitch to only a few batters.

coaches The men who assist the manager in running his team.
coaching box The boxes next to first and third base where the two base coaches stand to guide the offensive players.
count The total number of balls and strikes against a batter.
crack The sound of a baseball hitting a bat. *Delino was off with the crack of the bat.*
curveball A pitch that curves while traveling in the air.
cut A swing. *Rob took an enormous cut at that pitch.*
dead ball A temporary stop in play.
deliver 1. The act of a pitcher throwing to home plate. 2. Making a respected play. *Tray really delivered on that last play.*
delivery 1. A pitcher's throw to home plate. *Todd's delivery was just a bit outside.*
designated hitter A batter assigned by the manager to bat in place of the pitcher in the batting order.
DH Short for designated hitter.
dinger Slang for home run.
double header Two games played on the same day by the same two teams.
double steal An offensive play in which two runners attempt to steal bases at the same time.
double A hit in which a batter makes it safely to second base.
double-play A sequence of play in which two offensive players are called out.
DP a double play.
dug out The area where the players, managers and coaches sit when they are not on the field or in the bull pen.
early innings The first, second and third innings.
earned run Any run given up by a pitcher that is not the result of an error.
earned run average ERA A statistic computed by multiplying the total number of earned runs given up by a pitcher during the season by the number of innings (six to nine, depending on the league), and then dividing the total by the number of innings the pitcher is in the game.
extra innings Any inning after the ninth inning.
fair Any baseball hit by the batter that stays inside the foul lines between first and third base, or any hit baseball that first lands in the outfield.
fast ball A hard-thrown straight pitch.
field umpire An official who patrols the field.
fielder A defensive player.
fielding average A statistic computed for a fielder by dividing his total number of put-outs and assists by his total number of put-outs, assists and errors.

first base The base located on the right corner of the diamond-shaped playing field, looking out from home plate.
first baseman A defensive player who is positioned to the left of first base looking out from home plate.
fly ball A baseball hit upward in the air.
force out An out in which a baseball is thrown to a fielder touching a base to which a runner was forced to run.
fork ball Slang for split-fingered fast ball. *Jack has a nasty fork ball.*
foul Short for foul ball.
foul ball Any baseball hit that rolls outside of the foul lines between first and third base or hit directly into foul territories.
foul lines The lines that extend from home plate through both first and third base to the outfield wall.
foul poles The poles that divide fair territory from foul territory, located on the outfield wall.
foul tip A strike in which a baseball is fouled directly back into the catcher's mitt.
full count A count with three balls and two strikes against the batter.
gap An open area between two fielders. *Vinnie Vincenzo hit the ball right into the gap—Bill and Bob both missed it.*
gas Slang for a fastaball
glove A leather glove most fielders wear on their hand to help them catch the baseball.
gopher ball An untimely home run given up by a pitcher (maybe losing the game). *Mike served up a gopher ball.*
grab.Slang for catch.
grand salami Slang for grand-slam home run.
grand slam A home run hit with the runners on first, second and third bases.
ground ball A baseball hit that rolls on the ground.
ground out A ground ball thrown to a fielder touching a base before a runner gets there.
ground-rule double When a batted baseball lands anywhere on the field of play and then bounces out of play.
heater Slang for a fast ball.
hill The pitcher's mound.
hit and run When runner(s) start(s) running as the pitcher throws the baseball and the batter tries to hit the baseball into the open area of the infield left open by the fielder who moves to cover the base the runner(s) is trying to steal.
hit for the cycle To hit a single, double, triple and a home run in one game.

home plate The base located on the bottom of the diamond-shaped playing field, where the runners must touch to score runs.
home run When a batter hits a pitch over the outfield wall and is allowed to advance all the way to home plate.
home plate umpire The official who patrols home plate.
home team The team who bats second.
in the hole The place in the batting order in which a player bats after the player that bats after the batter.
infield fly rule The Rule in which a catchable fly ball is hit in the infield with fewer than two outs, with runners on first and second, or with the bases loaded, where the batter is automatically out.
infield The area located inside the 90-foot diamond-shaped playing field.
infielder A defensive player who is positioned in the infield.
inning The sections a baseball game is divided into.
inside The side of home plate closest to the batter.
inside the park home run The hit in which a runner makes it all the way to home plate on a baseball hit inside the playing field.
intentional walk A walk purposely given up by the pitcher.
k'd Slang for strike out.
knuckle ball knuckler. A pitch thrown with absolutely no spin.
late innings The seventh, eighth, and ninth innings.
lead off, -ing 1. To stand away from a base. 2. To be the first batter in an inning.
left field The left side of the outfield, looking out from home plate.
left fielder A defensive player who sands in left field.
lifetime statistics The measured statistics that are tallied over a lifetime.
light up the base path To steal many bases.
line drive A baseball hit low and hard in the air.
line up Slang for batting order.
lit up The description of a pitcher in which the batters are getting hits on almost every pitch he throws. *Mike Holt is getting lit up; I mean they're hitting everything.*
long ball Slang for home run.
loss A statistic credited to any pitcher who allows the opposing team to score enough runs to win the game.
manager The man who directs a team in games and practices.
meat Slang for player.
middle innings The fourth, fifth, and sixth innings.
middle reliever A relief-pitcher who pitches after the starting pitcher.
mitt A heavily padded leather glove that the catcher and first baseman wear to catch the baseball.

night cap The second game of a double-header.
nubber A hit baseball with little velocity.
number one The signal commonly used by the catcher, instructing the pitcher to throw a fast ball.
numbers Slang for statistics.
off the fists A pitch that hits the bat near a batter's hands.
off the hook A win in which a team is losing, then scores enough runs to prevent a pitcher from recording a loss.
official scorer The man who records and determines the scoring of a game.
on base percentage A statistic computed by dividing a batter's total number of hits, walks, and times hit by a pitch by his total number of at bats, walks, times hit by a pitch and sacrifices.
on deck The player who bats after the batter.
one-hopper A baseball that a fielder catches after it bounces once.
open base A base with no runner occupying it.
out of play The area beyond the foul territory when in which a baseball goes, it becomes a dead ball.
out of the park A home run hit over the outfield fence.
out The rule in which an offensive player loses his eligibility to stay on a base, and must leave the field.
outfield wall outfield fence. wall. fence. A wall at the far end of the outfield that varies in height and distance from home plate in various stadiums.
outfield The area of the field beyond the infield.
outfielder A defensive player who is positioned in the outfield.
outside The side of home plate away from the batter.
painting the corners See special section in Chapter 6 Here's the Pitch.
park Short for ball park.
passed ball A pitch not caught by the catcher, and not hit by the batter.
pen Short for bull pen
pepper games A form of practice played close together with a batter and five fielders, who work on catching softly hit baseballs.
pick off To get a runner out who is away from a base before a pitch has been thrown. *Dave was too far off the bag—he got picked off.*
pickle Slang for run down.
pinch hitter A batter that enters the game to hit for a batter in the batting order.
pinch runner A player who enters the game to run in place of a runner who is on base.
pitch The throws a pitcher makes to the batter.
pitcher The fielder who stands on the pitcher's mound and throws the

baseball for the other team to try to hit.
pitcher's mound The area in the center of the infield where the pitcher stands to throw the baseball to the batter.
pitcher's plate The plate in the middle of the pitcher's mound from which the pitcher must throw every pitch.
pitching coach The coach assigned to work with the pitchers on his team.
play ball The command given by the home plate umpire to start play
pop-up Slang for fly ball.
pulling the string Slang for strike out.
punch out slang. To strike a batter out.
put-out That which a fielder is credited if he catches the baseball to record an out.
rain maker A hit in which the baseball is hit extremely high.
RBI Runs batted in Anytime a batter walks, sacrifices, or gets a hit, and a run scores.
relievers The pitchers who replace the starting pitcher.
retire the side, -ing To get three outs.
right field The right side of the outfield.
right fielder A defensive player who is positioned in right field.
rook rookie A first year player.
round tripper Slang for home run.
rubber Slang for pitcher's plate.
run Points scored by a team.
rundown The situation in which a runner is caught running in between two bases.
ring up slang. To strike a batter out.
runner A player that safely reaches first, second, or third base.
runners on the corners The situation in which there are runners standing safely on first and third base only.
sacrifice When a batter hits the baseball, and moves at least one runner to the next base, but does not safely reach base himself.
sacs are full sacs full. The bases loaded.
safe Any time the runner or batter-runner does not have to leave the field.
save A statistic in which a relief-pitcher enters the game where his team leads by three or fewer runs, or has the potential tying run on base, at the plate, or on deck, and finishes the game without giving up more than two runs or comes into pitch well forthree innings with more than a three run lead.
screwball A pitch that goes from high to low in the air.
second base The base in the upper-middle of the diamond, looking out from home plate.

second baseman A defensive player who is positioned in between first and second base.
set position The description of how a pitcher begins his throw to home plate in which a pitcher starts his motion sideways to the batter, and at which point must come to a complete stop in his motion.
set up man A relief-pitcher who replaces the middle relief-pitcher.
seventh inning stretch The part of the seventh inning that is considered in the middle.
sharp A hard hit baseball.
shin guards The protective equipment catchers (and sometimes batters) wear on their shins.
shortstop A defensive player who stands in between second and third base.
shot 1. Slang for home run. 2. The description of a hit. *Boy, was that a great shot into center field.*
show Slang for Major Leagues.
shutout A team failing to score any runs.
single A hit in which a batter makes it safely to first base.
slide An attempt to get on base in which a runner dives feet first, or head first.
slider A pitch that sharply changes direction in the air.
slugger A successful batter.
slugging percentage A statistic computed by giving a batter one point for all the singles he has hit, two points for all the doubles, three points for all the triples, four points for all the home runs, and dividing the total combined number by his total number of at bats.
slump The time in which a batter has difficulty hitting the baseball, or a team has trouble winning games. *The River Rats are in a slump. They just can't win a game.*
smash 1. Slang for home run. 2. To hit the baseball hard.
smoke *smoker*. Slang for fast ball.
solo shot A home run hit with no runners on base.
south paw A left-handed pitcher.
split-fingered fast ball A dipping fast ball, with similar motion to the slider.
squeeze play A bunt on which a runner on third base steals home plate.
stance Short for batter's stance.
statistics The records of players' performances during the season.
stealing An offensive play in which a runner tries to advance to the next base when the pitcher is in the motion of pitching the baseball.
stopper A hard-throwing relief pitcher who pitches to only a few batters.
stretch The term commonly used for the pitcher's set position.

strike 1. A pitch the umpire rules hitable by the batter 2. a missed swing at the baseball by the batter.
strike zone The area that is half way between the batter's waist and shoulders to his knees, as measured when he is in his stance.
strike out the side,-ing To strike out three batters in one inning.
stuff Slang for pitches.
suicide squeeze Slang for squeeze play.
switch hitter A batter who can bat from either side of home plate.
tag up, -ing To advance on a sacrifice fly.
Texas leaguer A softly hit fly ball that lands in the outfield for a base hit.
third base The base in the left corner of the diamond, looking out from home plate.
third baseman A defensive player who is positioned to the right of third base, looking out from home plate.
third strike rule The rule in which a third strike is not called after a missed swing by a batter, where, if the catcher drops a third-strike pitch, the runner must be tagged or forced out.
top The half inning when the visiting team bats.
triple A hit in which a batter makes it safely to third base.
twin bill Slang for double header.
twin-killing Slang for double play.
umpires The officials who patrol specific regions on the field to assure that the players follow the rules.
up to bat The time that a batter goes into the batter's box to face the pitcher.
visiting team The team that bats first.
walk Slang for base on balls.
wall Short for outfield wall.
warning track A trade to warn an outfielder that he is close to the wall.
wear the collar, -ing To get no hits in five at bats in one game.
whiff To swing and miss. A strike. *What a whiff by George.*
wild pitch A pitch not caught by the catcher, that is the result of a wild throw made by the pitcher.
win A statistic that credits the pitcher who was the last player to pitch for his team when the winning run was scored.
wind up The description of how a pitcher begins his throw to home plate in which a pitcher starts his motion facing the batter, and at which point does not have to come to a complete stop in his motion.
wood The contact part of a hit, usually signifying a hard hit. *Ruby got some wood on the ball that time. It went to the wall.*

Index

G-H

I

L-M

T

U-V-W

Win a Pair of Tickets to See *Your* Favorite Major League® Team Play†

complete with transportation

Enter your name, address, city, state, zip code and phone number in the spaces provided below. Then, tear this page out of the book, and return it to:

AARON'S BOOKS
P.O. Box 4241
Ann Arbor, Michigan 48106

Name:________________________

Address:______________________

City:__________ State:__________

Zip Code:________Phone:__________

Favorite Team:

† Restricted to regular season games played in the continental United States, Toronto, or Montreal.

No purchase necessary. For a free entry form, or a complete listing of entry rules write to Aaron's Books, P.O. Box 4241, Ann Arbor, MI, 48106. Entries must be received by July 15, 1993. All requests are subject to availability. All persons entered must 18 years of age or older, or must be accompanied by a parent or legal guardian.